I0420040

Ocean Animal Pattern

Coloring Book for Adults

An Adult Coloring Book Of 40 Ocean Pattern Coloring Pages in a Range of Stress Relieving Patterns

Adult Coloring World

ISBN-13: 978-1522799368

ISBN-10: 1522799362

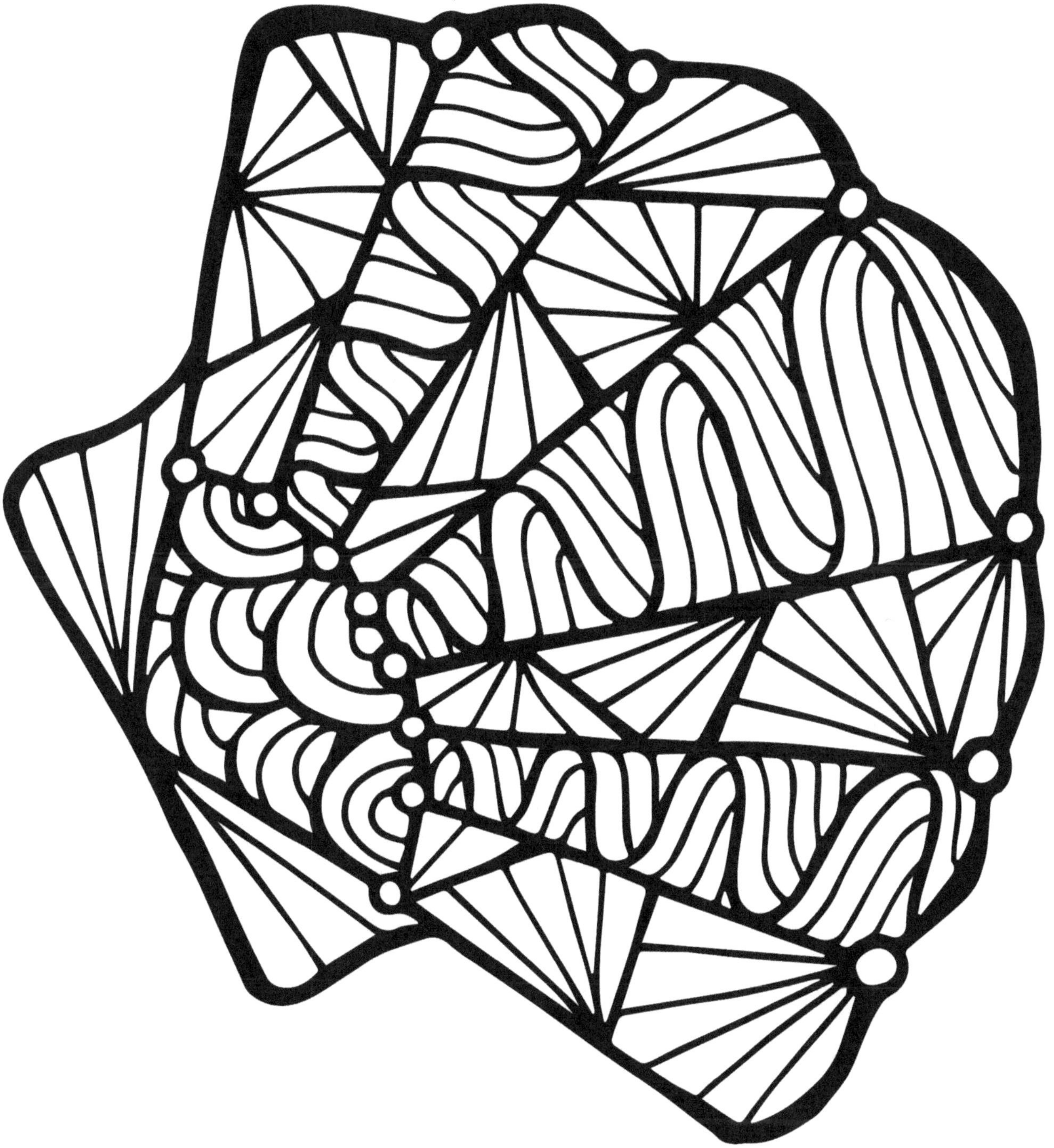

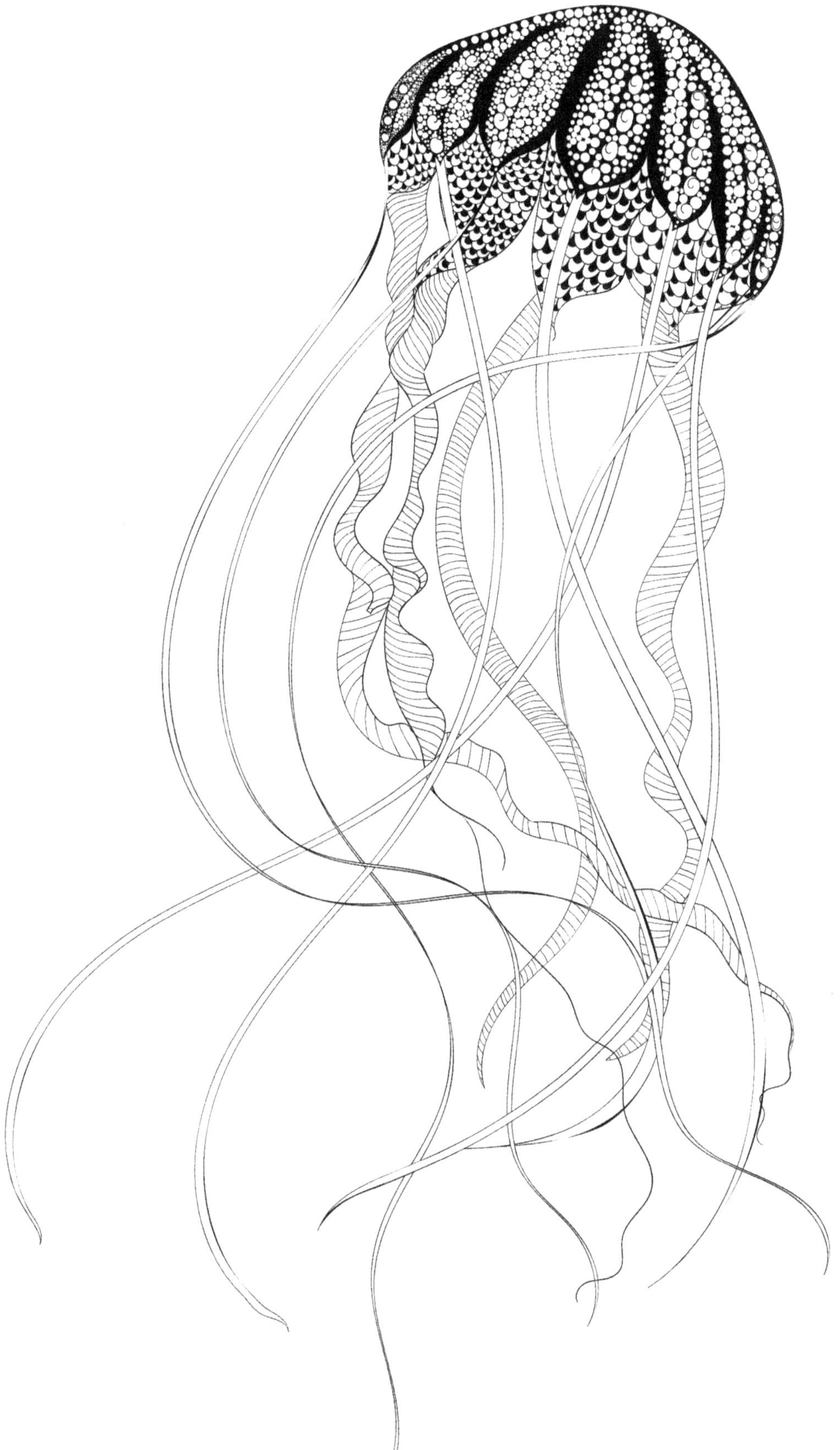

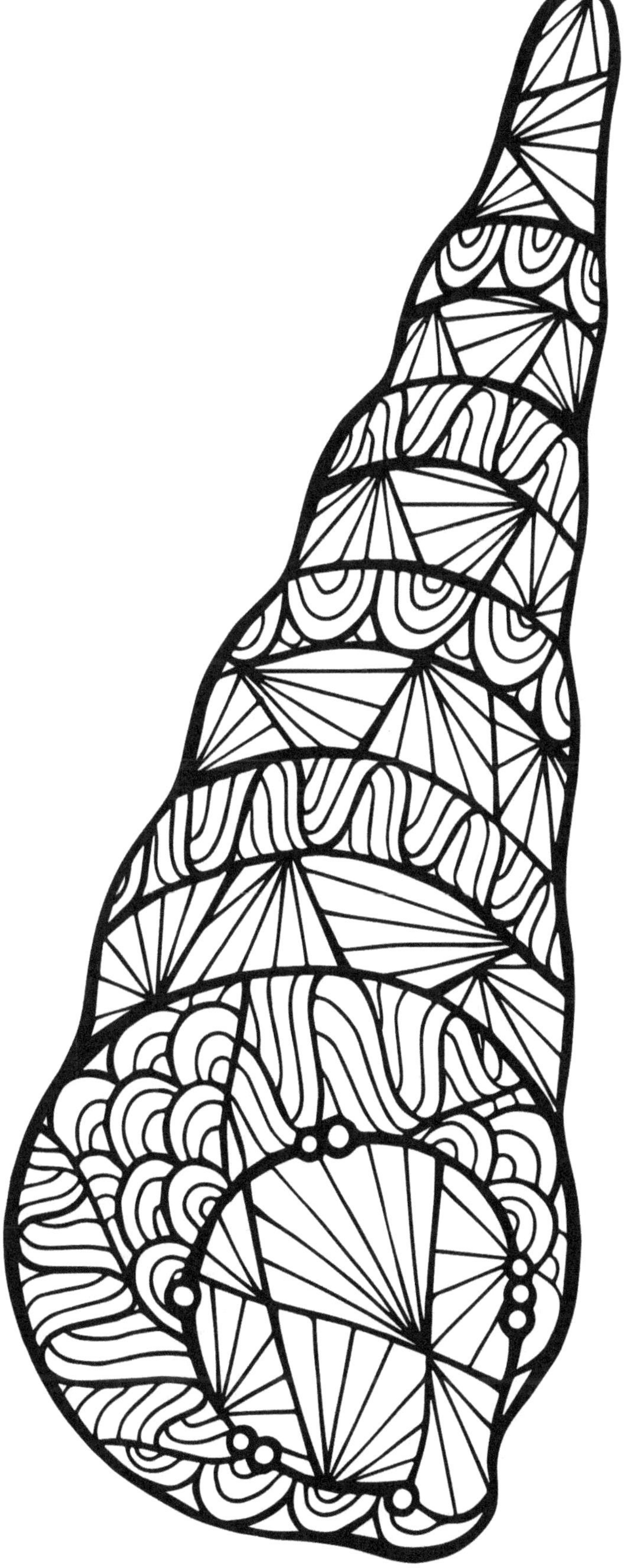

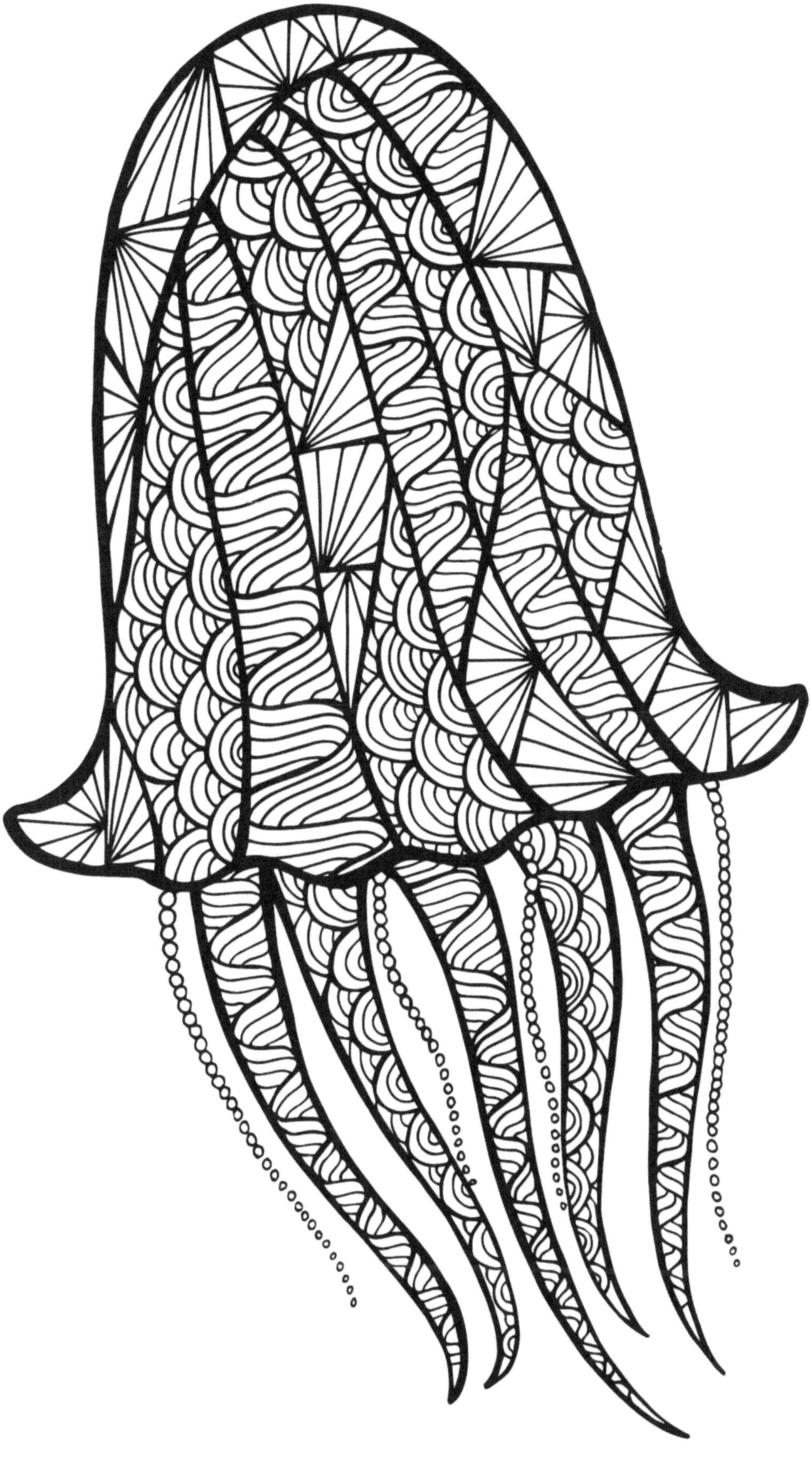

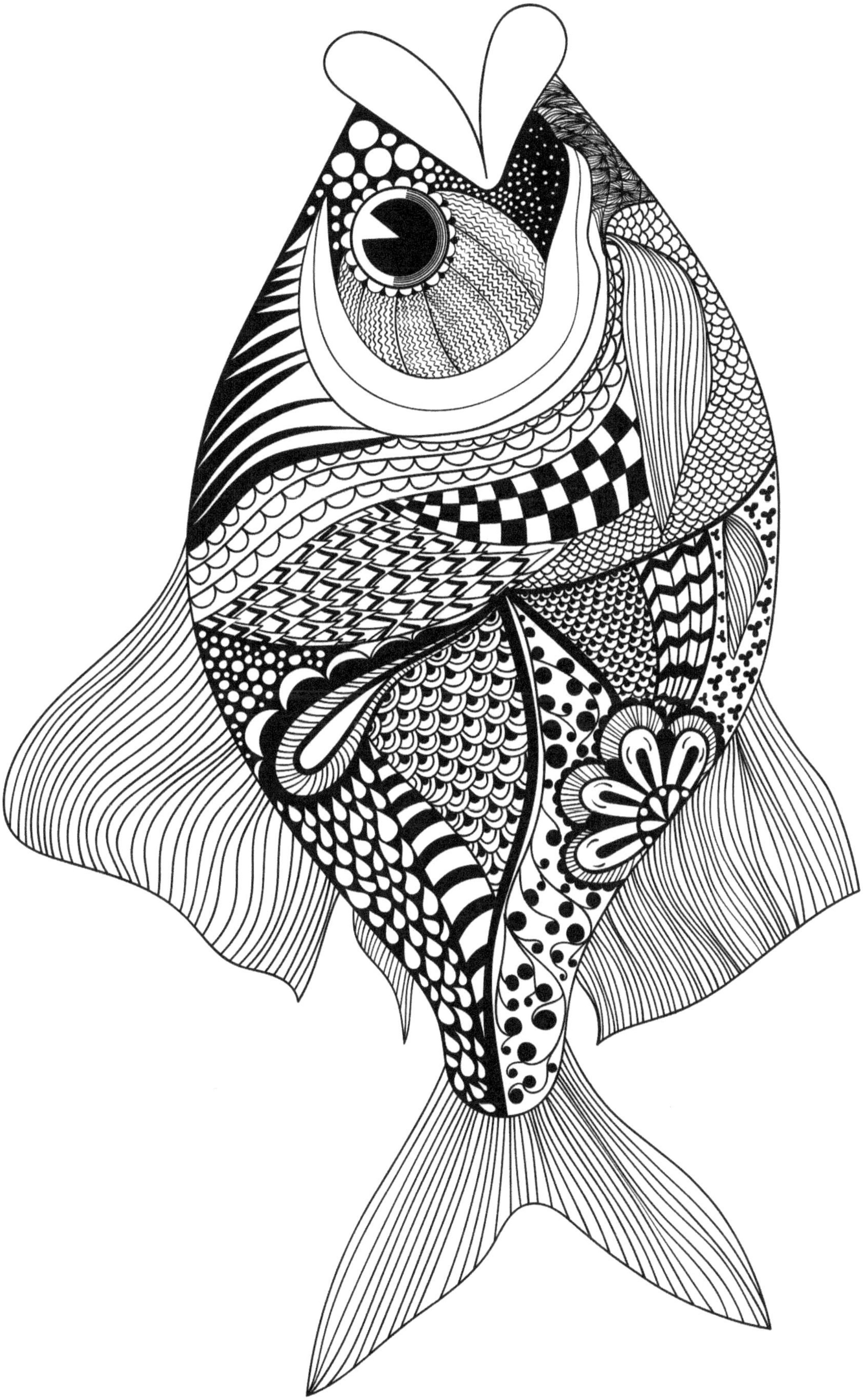

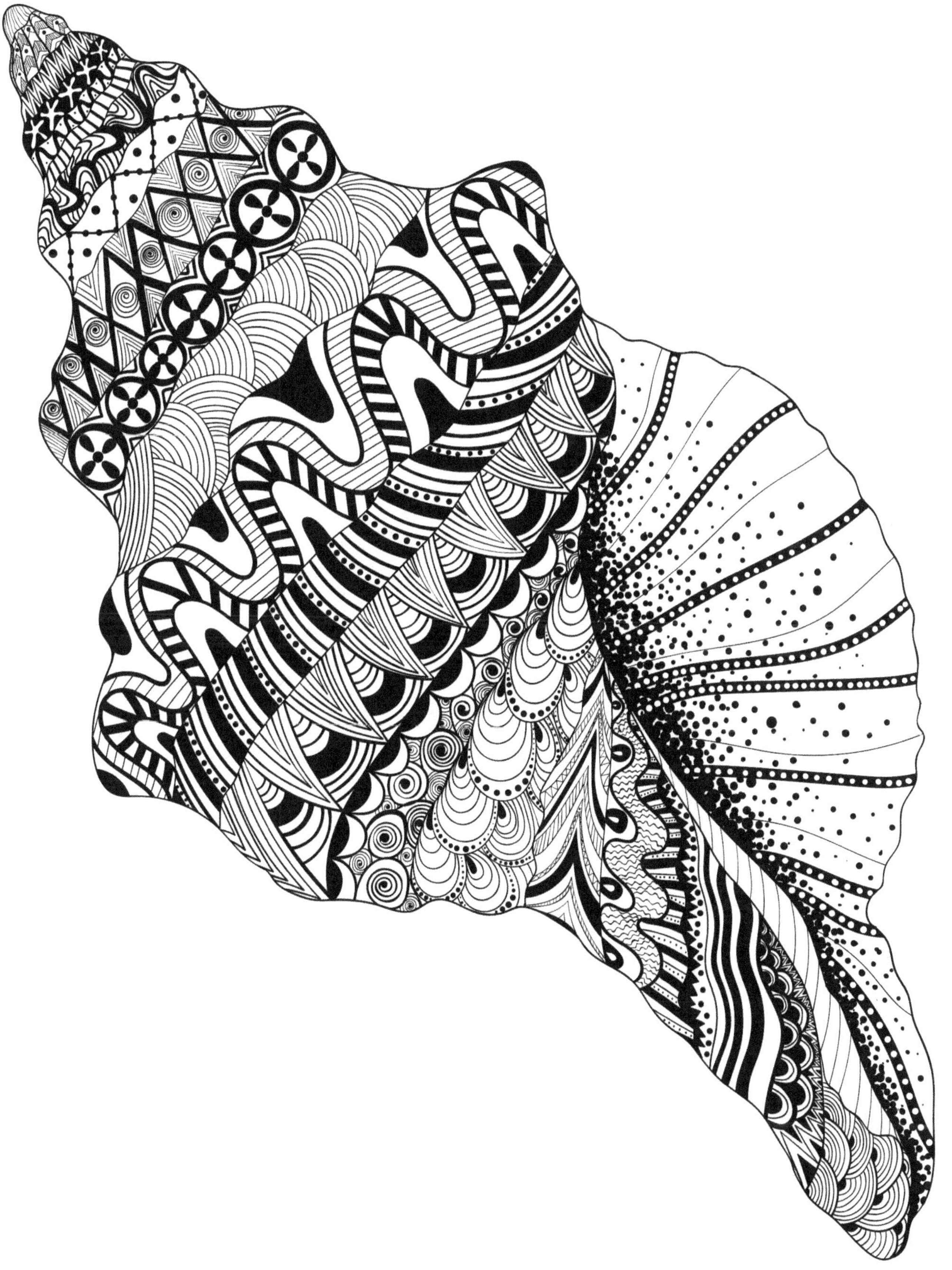

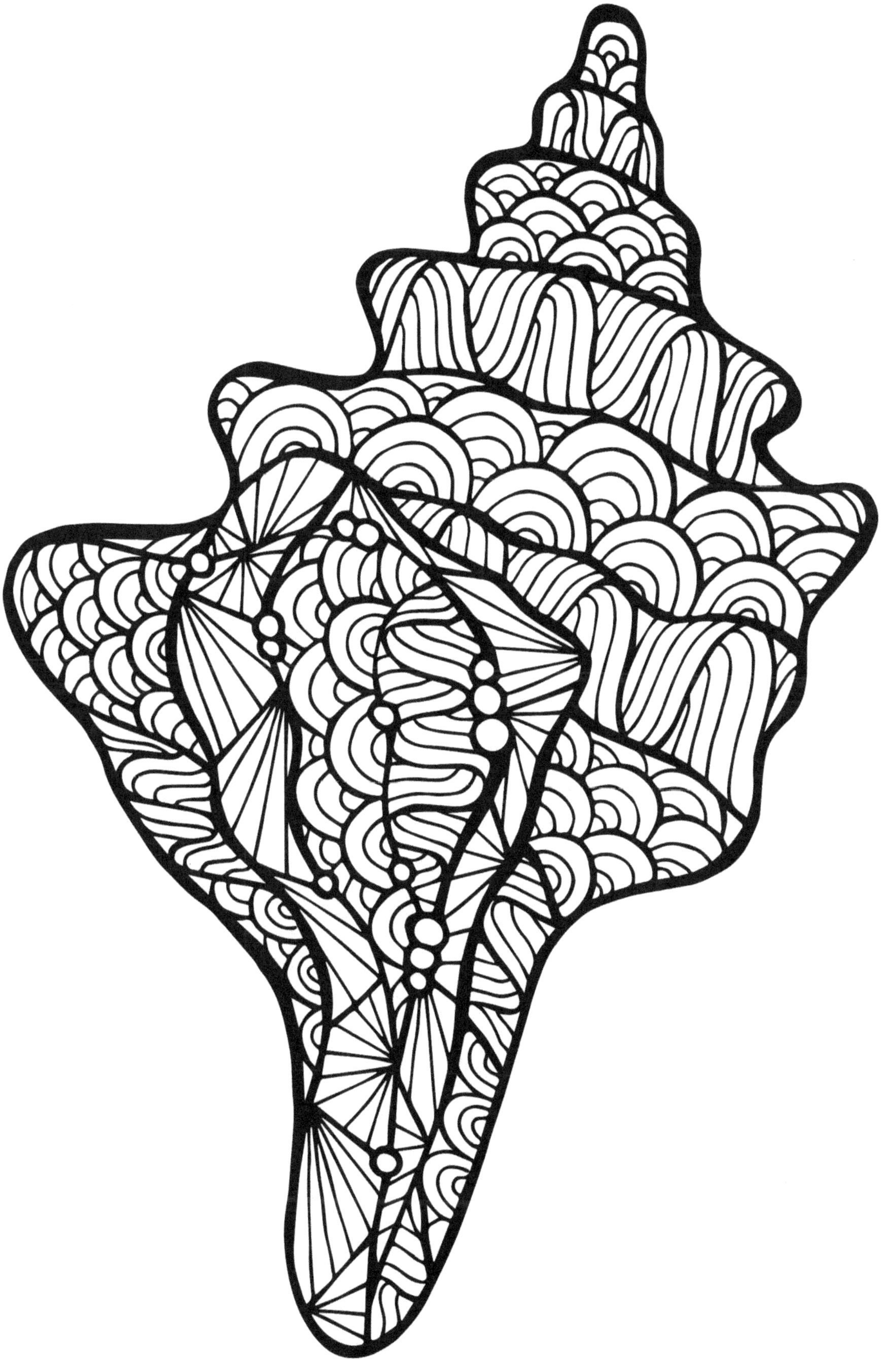

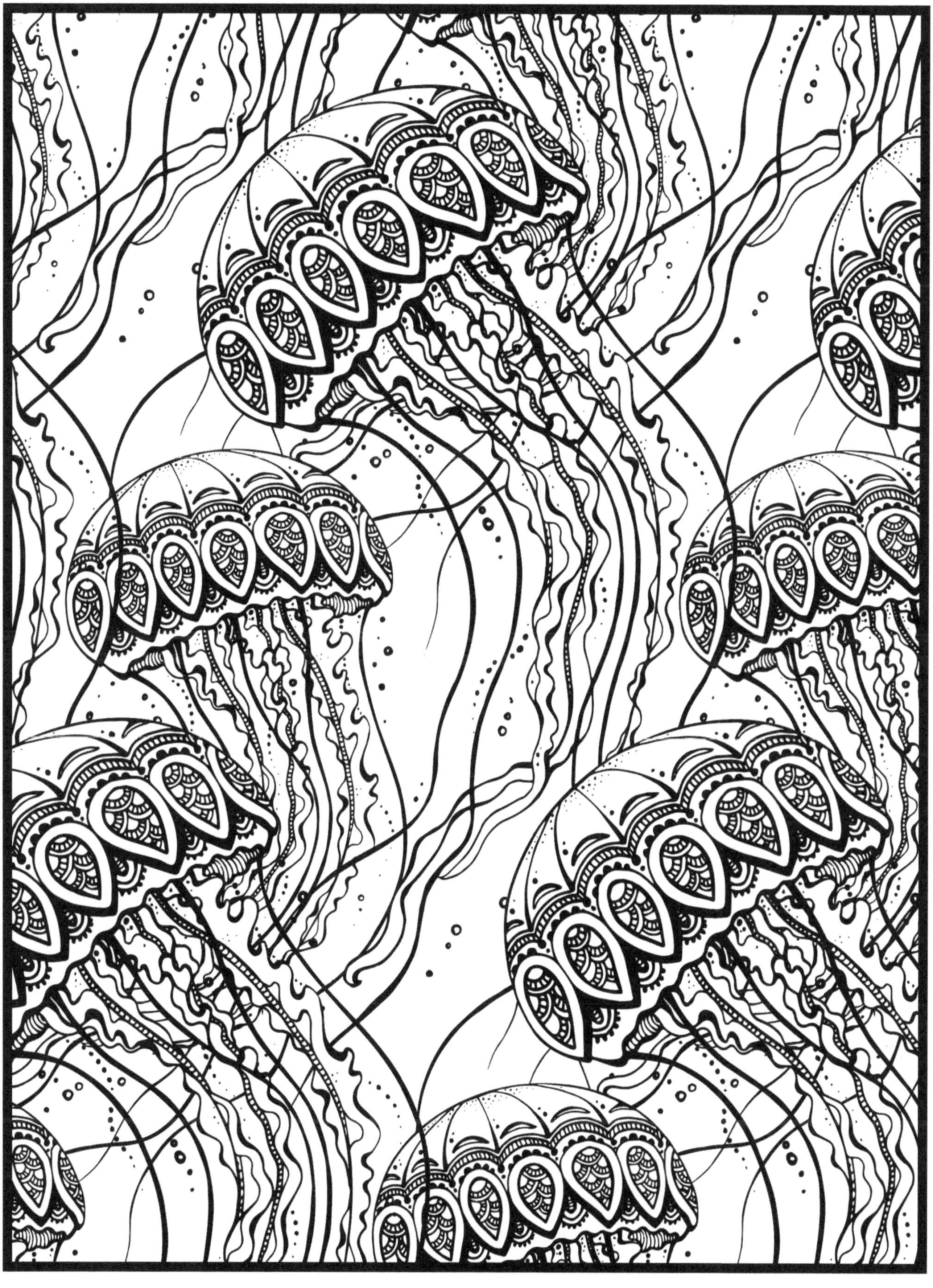

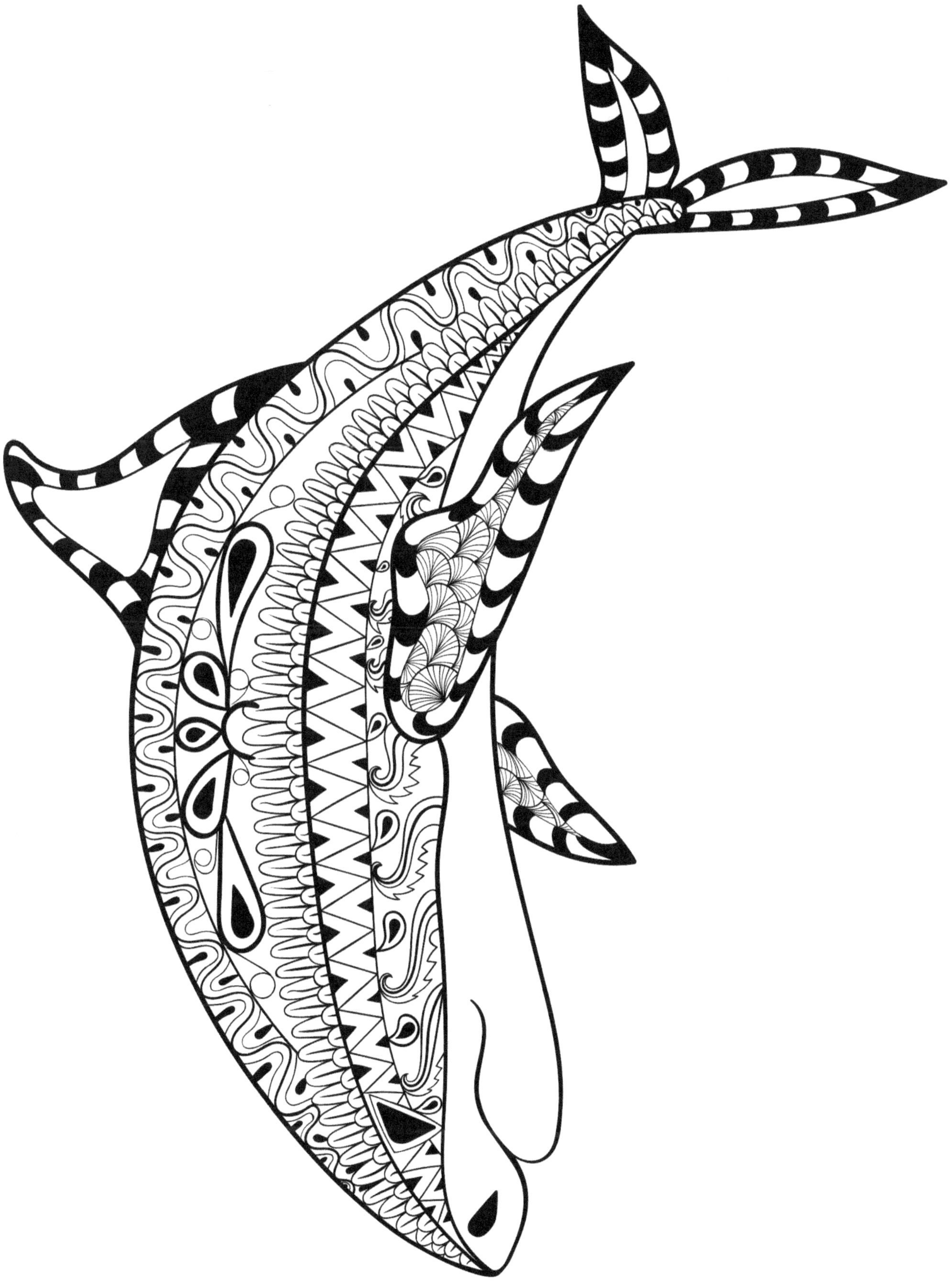

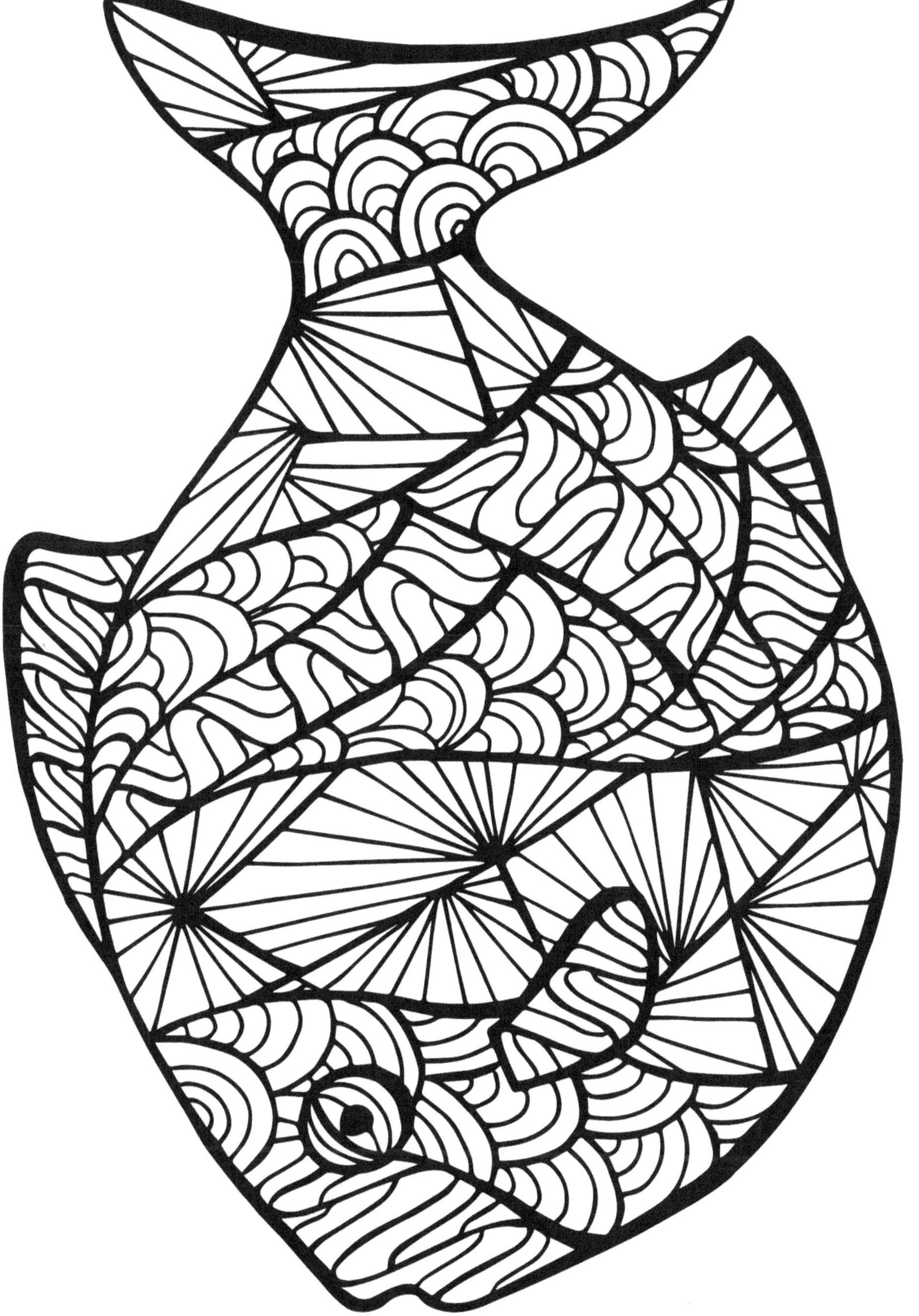

www.ingramcontent.com/pod-product-compliance
Lightning Source LLC
Chambersburg PA
CBHW081235280526
45787CB00006B/2671
9781522799368